Love Covers:

10 Tips to Ignite Healthy Relationships

LaKeesha Hines, CPLC

ISBN 978-1-7320008-0-3

Published by

Emerge Publishing Group, LLC
Riviera Beach, FL
www.emergepublishers.com

LaKeesha Hines, 2018
Love Covers: 10 Tips to Ignite Your Relationship
1. Family 2. Marriage 3. Parenting

Printed in the United States of America

Contents

Dedication

I would like to dedicate this book to God first. Without him, this book would never have been written. It was He who inspired and instructed me to do so. The experiences and lessons He allowed me have led me to become the wife, friend, and mother I am today.

My husband…my rock, comforter, lover, and friend…this life would be miserable without you. The trials, tribulations, and TRIUMPHS of married life would not have been learned without you.

Lastly, this book is dedicated to Pastor Mohead. We are eternally grateful to you for teaching us that love truly covers.

About the Igniter

LaKeesha is a wife and mother of four extraordinary and gorgeous children. Through the course of her life, she has learned valuable lessons which she will share with you. LaKeesha has a Bachelor's degree in Psychology and a Master's degree in School Counseling. She has worked in her local school district as a Parent Liaison assisting parents of children with special needs with navigating the system and advocating for their children. She is a Psychology instructor at a local college and Certified Professional Life Coach passionate about helping people overcome any obstacles preventing them from leading happy, healthy lives.

The Spark

This book was written to provide tips for re-igniting the passion in marriages, maintaining healthy friendships, and improving parent/ child relationships. If you aren't married, that's okay. This can be used to prevent your marriage from needing re-ignition. MARRIAGE IS HARD! It takes hard work, dedication, and commitment. Maintaining happy, healthy marriages becomes increasingly difficult when children are thrown into the mix and even more challenging if one or more of them has a disability(ies). If you're ready for ignition, allow me to show you how applying the concept of two simple words will change your entire life!

The Ignition

I am a mother of four children ranging in development from early childhood to adolescence at the time this book was written. I have been married to my phenomenal husband for 10 years, but have known him since elementary school. Through the course of our 10 years of marriage, I have learned beyond valuable life lessons which God urged me to share with you. Having a BA in Psychology has given me a greater understanding of people and how their minds work. Having a MA in School Counseling and working in my local school district as a Parent Liaison has given me a greater understanding of the challenges parents who have children with special needs face. I am extremely

passionate about helping couples to overcome any-
and-all obstacles or barriers which prevent them
from leading happy, healthy lives. Fulfilling your
passion and receiving the desires of your heart as
you share your life with others romantically and
platonically is one of my number one goals for your
life. My prayer is that you will be blessed by this
book and begin to live the abundant life God
designed especially for you.

Over the course of my marriage, I have
experienced significant ups and downs within my
faith, family, and finances. My husband and I have
one child with multiple disabilities resulting from
two strokes and several seizures caused by a bout
with bacterial meningitis during infancy. We had,
and still do have such a major financial burden
caring for a child with special needs. But, God

continues to provide and make a way out of NO way! I questioned God about allowing the trajectory of my son's life to be completely transformed by meningitis. I spent a significant amount of time in denial about my son's diagnoses, feeling angry and depressed about his new life, and bargaining with God to "fix" him. If you are familiar with the stages of grief, you know that is exactly what I went through. Grieving occurs after a loss. I was grieving the loss of my vision and dream for my son's life and future.

My faith was truly tested as I had the horrific opportunity to watch my son stop breathing and be resuscitated twice during a six-week stay in the hospital as he battled meningitis. But, God! My then, on-again, off-again boyfriend and I were in a long-distance relationship. Having a child with significant disabilities taught us to value the small things in life, brought us closer together, and ultimately closer to God. Not only did my boyfriend decide to become my husband (due to direct instruction from God), but he also dropped everything, left Georgia, and moved to Florida to get his family together.   God turned tragedy into triumph! There were times when my husband and I truly could not stand to be in the same room together let alone continue to be married. But, God! I was traditionally attracted to men because of their physical characteristics (along with their level of intelligence, achievements, etc.). But now, there is nothing more attractive to me than a man who listens and obeys God. My husband is easy on my eyes too!

Through the course of my marriage, I have learned a multitude of things. Some were extremely profound and others simple, yet powerful. Before my husband and I got married, we had a tumultuous time. We were both trying to finish college which is why we were in a long-distance relationship. I was a single mom with one child from a previous relationship, working full-time and going to school. It was difficult, but we made the best of it. When our son became ill with meningitis, we both blamed ourselves. We had issues with family members on both sides creating more conflict than resolution.

When God spoke to my husband and told him that I was to be his wife, we were not in a good place. We had broken up and really didn't like each other. But, with time and allowing God to heal us individually and collectively, we forgave one another, and ultimately ourselves. We learned how to give our family members over to God and allow

Him to handle it. All parties involved had to acknowledge the roles they played in the discord. We let the past be the past. All of this did not come second nature or come easy to us. We decided that pre-marital counseling would be best for us if we had any hope of making it down the aisle and staying together for the long haul after the promissory "I do's."

You aren't going to believe me when I tell you this, but we went to three different pastoral counselors. One of the counselors was most like a professor. We attended classes for six weeks, we had a workbook, in-class discussions with other engaged couples, and guidance from the pastor. It was great! It forced us to discuss some of our pet peeves, individual expectations of marriage, and to be committed to stay together no matter what…the 'D' word was not an option! The other pastor was prophetic. She could hear from God like no one I have ever known. She was very spiritual and knew the Word of God like no one's business! We learned that if we kept God first, everything else would fall into place. She taught us the importance of praying for each other, praying together for our marriage, and praying over our children. She ultimately was the one who presided over our wedding.

The last pastor (the *first* pastor we saw) was very quiet, meek, patient, and kind. She gave us one simple piece of information...Love covers. When she said that to us, we both looked at each other and frowned. Love covers? Love covers! That's it?! That's all?! You don't have anything else to tell us? Oh boy, we're doomed, we thought. "Love covers" is not going to cover all this mess we have going on between us, within our families, and with our child with special needs. We needed more. So, we sought out more help from the other two pastors previously mentioned. We learned something from all three of them and each one was phenomenal in their own rights. But, I would be remiss if I did not tell you after 10 years of marriage, I finally get what "love covers" truly means. It took me this long to get it, hopefully not as long for you. "Love covers" is actually a small, yet extremely powerful, part of a scripture found in the Bible. Proverbs 10:12 in the New International Version of the Bible says, "Hatred stirs up conflict, but love covers over all wrongs."

Does this mean that you ignore any and every act your spouse does that is hurtful to your or upsets you? Absolutely, not! But, what it does mean is that you don't harp on the transgressions. You trust that the person you love, loves you back and would never do anything to intentionally hurt or upset you. It means, not thinking of your spouse as being against you. It means choosing to see the good in them and not focusing on what's going wrong. It also means choosing to just flush the toilet and keep quiet when you go to use it and your spouse forgot to flush after using it, instead of complaining to them about it.

My husband and I were in such a bad space when we met with the "love covers" pastor. We were still so angry with one another and our wounds were still open and raw. I think we were even angry with God for telling us that it was His will for us to be together! We couldn't see past all the hurt, anger, and hate. As mentioned previously, we didn't even like each other. We were no longer attracted to one another physically, mentally, or emotionally. But,

God! To get to a healthy, happy place took time, prayer, forgiveness, fasting, patience, abstinence, commitment, faith, hope, and love. On our wedding day, we were truly in love! We couldn't wait to say I do. It was magical, spiritual, emotional, and beautiful. A true testament to God's awesome wisdom, power, and love. Today, we can't see how we would make it without each other and our family is stronger than ever.

When our son was in the hospital with meningitis, none of my close friends came. They called and checked in periodically, but no one came. I even received a meal once or twice, but no one physically came and sat with me in the hospital room as I remained at my son's bedside. Even after we went home, some didn't come. This made me re-evaluate my relationships with my friends. In one of my most desperate hours the people I felt I should have been able to lean on were not there for me and it hurt. It took years for my friends and I to discuss this. But, when we did, love covered! I was able to forgive them because they acknowledged, accepted, and apologized for their part. Now, we are all closer than ever before. I also had to acknowledge my part which was that I did not make my needs, wants, or expectations known. I had to seek forgiveness as well.

The tips I will share with you in the following pages are all life lessons that I learned along the way and still reference today. I do not claim to be the resident expert. However, I am sharing what has worked for me within my marriage, friendships, and in my relationships with my children. I pray you are blessed and that you will ignite or re-ignite the passion in your relationships.

Laugh Until Combustion

"A time to weep, and a time to laugh; a time to mourn, and a time to dance;" - Ecclesiastes 3:4 (KJV)

A good laugh can make you temporarily forget whatever you are going through during a particularly unpleasant moment in time. I remember being so upset with my husband during an argument and then he did something silly. I was so angry with him that I tried to contain my laughter, but it was so funny that I had to let go and out it came... COMBUSTION! I laughed so hard, in fact that I almost urinated on myself. After the laughter was over, I tried to recall what we were arguing about. I remembered what it was, but then said to myself, "this isn't even worth it!"

Now, am I suggesting that everything can be resolved with a laugh? Certainly not. However, I am suggesting that there is healing in laughter. It can make you feel better when you are sad. Timed right, laughter can help you remember not to sweat the small stuff. Laughter can also help you to focus on the things that truly matter...love, joy, peace, etc.

If you don't happen to have a comedian living under your roof, you might have to get a little creative. Try to remember something silly that you or someone you know did. Think about a good joke you heard at work that left you in stitches. You can do an internet search for jokes on the internet or look up You Tube videos of your favorite comedian. Don't be afraid to make a fool of yourself by acting silly for the betterment of your relationship. Make funny faces or do a silly dance.

Sometimes we get to a place where we find ourselves unhappy. That unhappiness could be due to excess weight gained, loss of a loved one, job stress, financial strain or a disconnected relationship with your spouse. Of course, there are a myriad of other causes. What I think we are all guilty of at some point is taking ourselves and things too seriously. Sometimes we just need to laugh at ourselves. While stopping for a moment to laugh won't make our problems go away, it will help them seem just a wee bit smaller.

Look in your phone at your text messages. How often do you see "LOL" show up? LOL, or "laugh(ing) out loud," has become a movement. Almost everyone on the planet knows what it means. It is a wonderful thing. One day just out of curiosity I decided to google the effects of laughing out loud. I came across so many positive reasons why it's a great idea, from boosting our immune systems to releasing endorphins in the brain. The one reason I enjoyed the most was laughing out loud makes us happy. I don't know about you but one of the main reasons why I enjoy hanging out with my friends is because I know I am going to get at least one really, really good laugh. The same way laughter decreases the tension in a marital relationship, it can do the exact same for our friendships. Even when I have had conflict in one of my friendships, once we dealt with the issue at hand we were able to look back later and laugh about it.

Having multiple children of various age groups can be tough. From my hormonal teenager to my rambunctious kids in early childhood, their needs are all different. At times, there is conflict and differences of opinion. But, the one thing that is universal in this household with all their unique needs is laughter. They all enjoy laughing and making others laugh. They all respond to their dad and I being silly. I grew up in a home with very serious parents and I do not recall them ever really being silly with us outside of occasionally playing board games. In turn, I became a very serious adult. This is one of the reasons I believe God chose my husband for me. He was the balance that I needed in that he is so silly, loves to make people laugh, and knows how to let loose and just have fun. I am thankful that we are raising our kids in a home full of laughter.

Opponents Don't Win

"A hot-tempered man stirs up strife, but he who is slow to anger and patient calms disputes. -

Proverbs 15:18 (AMP)

When the word "opponent" was searched online, the definition found was, "someone who competes against or fights another in a contest, game, or argument; a rival or adversary." When you are competing against or fighting one another you cannot move toward a positive solution. When one of you become a rival or adversary, you become an enemy. An enemy is someone who does not have the other's best interest at heart, but instead are focused on their own wants and needs. The focus can easily become winning the argument versus what the argument is truly about.

Another definition for opponent located within the same internet search was, "A person who disagrees with or resists a proposal or practice." Let's just focus on the "practice" part of that definition. If one person is in the practice of walking away to avoid escalating an argument and the other likes to continue to push or attempt to force the other to continue to engage in the argument, there will be conflagration. Resisting the positive practice of taking a break before things get too heated is counterproductive and only makes matters worse.

Over the years, I discovered that I don't enjoy cleaning the bathroom. However, when I do clean it, I am very thorough. I take my time and am very detailed ensuring all the places that most people will never see are clean like the back of the commode. No one seemed to appreciate how detailed I was. There were no "thank you's" or comments about how clean it was. In fact, my husband would sometimes seem to be frustrated by how long it would take me to clean. My husband loves to serve his family. So, in an attempt to serve by helping around the house, cut the cleaning time in half, and because he knew I hated to do it, he decided to start cleaning the bathroom. He did a pretty good job, but he did not clean the bathroom the way I did. He did not clean behind the commode! I completely lost it!! HOW CAN YOU SAY THE BATHROOM IS CLEAN IF YOU DO NOT CLEAN BEHIND THE TOILET??!! Besides, that's what my mom taught me, so it has to be right. Right?!

The first time he did not clean behind the toilet I took a deep breath and looked away. The second time I looked away, but let out a huge huff. The third time, I exploded! He was so caught off guard by me that he didn't even know how to respond. Once he gathered himself, he asked me what was the big deal because no one could see back there; therefore, they would never know. That sent me through the roof. I said to him, "I KNOW!" He was so frustrated with me because of my lack of appreciation for his attempt to please and help me, that he finally yelled back at me. "ARE YOU PLANNING TO EAT BACK THERE? DO YOU TYPICALLY TOUCH ANYTHING BACK THERE OR IS ANYTHING BACK THERE TOUCHING ANY PART OF YOUR BODY??!!" I took a deep breath. I was angry because he yelled at me–which he typically never does because he is very quiet and laid back–even though I yelled at him first. But, I thought about the questions he asked me and I realized the answer to all three of his questions was no. Then, it was as if God hit a switch and a light came on. He is upset because he does not feel appreciated; the same way I had felt when no one commented on how great of a job I did. This situation also taught me about the volcano effect, which we will discuss later. Pick and choose your battles...not everything has to be addressed. But, if it is something that *truly* bothers you, it should be discussed with your spouse in a loving manner before it gets out of hand.

So now, let's break this scenario down. I hated cleaning the bathroom, so my husband decided to do it. When I cleaned it, I did not feel my detailed work was appreciated. When my husband cleaned it, he did not feel appreciated. All I wanted to do was make the bathroom nice for my family and all my husband wanted to do was help. Instead of seeing him as a *devoted* husband, I saw him as a *deficient* opponent. Instead of thanking him for his help, I hurt his heart. His heart and intentions were pure, and my need for perfection discouraged him and told him that he nor his efforts were sufficient. So, I asked myself whether the back of the commode being clean was worth the damage I did to my partner, my friend, my lover, my gift from God. The answer was clear...NO! So, I repented... apologized...and thanked my husband for appreciating me enough to help me around the house after working a full-time job. He forgave me and still chose to continue to clean the bathroom whenever I was too tired or just couldn't seem to get to it. He began making the effort of remembering to clean behind the commode. There were times he would forget. Do you know what I did? I shut up! I thanked him for helping to keep our home clean and kept it moving. Other times, I quietly cleaned it myself when he wasn't around so that he would not feel inadequate or unappreciated.

We both had the same goal which was to help and make our spouse happy. It's just that how we went about doing it was different.

There are going to be times when couples do not agree. This is totally normal and healthy. What is unhealthy is refusal to respect one another's view points and not trying to work together to move toward a solution. If both parties are focused on their own individual agendas or satisfying their own individual needs, there can be no resolution. OPPONENTS DO NOT WIN! Opponents are like two sticks being rubbed together over and over. Eventually they spark a flame and can cause conflagration.

Bringing things from our childhood and/ or past relationships can also cause conflagration. Just because our parents taught us how to do things a certain way does not automatically make that way the right way or the best way. When we refuse to let go of some of these prior teachings or allow ourselves to learn a new or different way, conflagration can occur. Conflagration can destroy a great deal of land. Don't become opponents and destroy the relationship (land) that you have worked so hard to build.

Growing up I constantly made friends with other females who were takers. They tried to take my boyfriend, my best friend, my belongings, etc. Additionally, there always seemed to be some sort of competition that only one of us was in and it wasn't me. I didn't care about trying to be the smartest or prettiest. I was just happy to have someone to laugh, play, and spend time with. On the contrary, my friends always wanted to pick the activity and only wanted to spend time with me when it was convenient for them, i.e. their boyfriend was busy. I learned the hard way that opposite agendas make opponents. If you and your friend are not on the same page or seeking the same things in the relationship, it will not work.

As I became an adult, the competition piece became more apparent. Our society teaches us what beauty is and what success looks like too. We are all being spoon-fed this mentality of getting ahead somehow requiring someone being stepped on to get there. This competition can be viewed in the board room and in the dressing room. Many have ended years of friendship because of back-stabbing behavior or belittling others to make oneself feel better. People often look down on others because they cannot afford brand named items. Instead of acceptance, they dish out ridicule when their success catapults them into a different tax bracket. Instead of carrying their friends along, they leave them behind. This is not always the case. Sometimes the successful friend does bring their friends along and because of jealously due to their lack of success they turn their back on the very person who tried to share their new lives with them.

If you are experiencing conflict in your friendship with someone regularly, it may be time to take a moment to evaluate that relationship. Do you or your friend have an unhealthy competitive spirit? If there jealously or envy? The two of you should spend some time discussing needs, wants, and expectations for one another. Perhaps you are not on the same page and the relationship has run its course. It also could be that there has been a misunderstanding along the way that just needs to be cleared up. We are so much more powerful when we stick together. In the end, opponents do not win.

Victory for All

If possible, as far as it depends on you, live at

peace with everyone." – Romans 12:18 (AMP)

It does not matter who wins during an argument.

When one party is happy, both parties win.   As

couples, we should be so focused on pleasing our

mate, it should be difficult finding time to focus on

winning or on who is right and who is wrong. I remember a time in my marriage where I was complaining to my husband about increasing our romance. He just never seemed to get it. I would do things for him that I wanted him to do for me and he never seemed to appreciate it. That frustrated me so much. I continued to do the exact same thing for years with no change.

Finally, one day I came across Gary Chapman's book, *The Five Love Languages,* and I learned what each of our love languages were. I was speaking to my husband using my primary love languages, gifts and quality time, instead of using his love language, acts of service. When I began to use his love language, I began noticing a change. There was a shift in the level of happiness within my husband which, in turn, caused him to want to speak my love language.

Not only did I use love languages, but I also began to pray and ask God for His help. Marriage is truly God's design and if we want it to be successful, we must follow His blue print. So, I began to pray for patience for myself because I knew that God needed time to work on both of us. I also prayed that God would give my husband a spirit of giving. Lastly, the prayer included asking God to show me ways in which I could perform acts of service for my husband along with the strength and energy to carry them out.

I began to lower my expectations because I knew that my love language did not come naturally to my husband, so he would need time to work on it. Lowering my expectations does not mean that I lowered my standards. It just means that it was unfair for me to expect my husband to be me! At one point, I felt that he should just *know* what I wanted and what I liked. That was a totally unrealistic and unfair way of thinking.

So, I tried to focus on just being appreciative and acknowledging any effort made on his part without criticism. The "without criticism" part is critical. If you constantly criticize or find something wrong with the effort your spouse makes, they might get discouraged and cease trying altogether due to feelings of insufficiency. I also stopped keeping score. It was no longer tit for tat. I am doing this because you did that. We gave and poured into each other and our marriage because of our love for each other, because it was the right thing to do and so that

God would be pleased. Thus, there was victory for all. Victory for all equals no conflagration!

This holds true for any relationship. Learning my friends' love languages and them learning mine was so beneficial to us. I understand them better and they understand me better. In the past, I would get one of my close girlfriends a gift for her birthday. She always appreciated it, but I could tell it didn't make her feel overjoyed. After learning "quality time" is her love language, I realized that she feels loved when we just hang out at her house together. Also, she is more of an introvert while I am more extroverted. Because of my "gift" love language, I was loving her the way I wanted to be loved. After years of friendship, we now know how to show one another love. When I want to love on her, we spend quality time together and when she wants to love on me, she gets me a gift. Getting to know what sets your friends off and what sets them on cloud nine is essential in any healthy, happy relationship.

Our relationship with our kids is no different. Learning each of our kids love languages is critical to their happiness. Each child is different and unique, so they should be treated as such. According to Mr. Chapman, small children will need equal components of all five love languages to ensure healthy development.

Enjoy Each Other's Company

"Live in harmony with one another;" –

Romans 12:16

There have been many couples who got married at a young age and managed to stay together well into late adulthood. But, are they happy? There has been so much research to support the fact that married couples become less content in their marriage after retirement. Some researchers attribute this lack of marital satisfaction to spending *too* much time together. However, the funny thing is, when we are younger we desire to spend ALL our time together. I agree with this, but only to a point. May I offer that it is not about the quantity of time, but the quality of it? Most people work hard during the prime of their lives and look forward to retirement. The problem is that couples become so focused on building a career and family that they forget to continue working on the relationship with their spouses. Thus, after retirement when couples finally can spend ALL their time together, they don't want to. They scramble to find things to do alone to get away from their spouse because they argue all the time or have nothing in common anymore. Couples must train themselves to continue throughout the marriage to enjoy one another's company like when they first met.

Because my husband and I have four children, it is extremely difficult to find time alone. It takes work...intentional effort...and much planning. At one point when our child with special needs was especially fragile, it was not just about finding the time. It was also about finding the energy. We were so physically and emotionally drained from caring for him that we stopped caring for ourselves and each other. But, help was on the way. We were blessed to find someone who could help us to care for him...to give us a break. So, we began having weekly date nights.

At first, our dates were exciting because we had not been "out" together in so long that we could not wait to find out what we had been missing! But, because it had been so long, we forgot how to just be around each other and have fun. We were so focused on the activity, the location, and making sure that everything was perfect that we ended up not having a good time at all. Week after week, each date got worse. We began to dread date night as it began to feel like a chore, instead of the highlight of our week. We began to argue about unimportant things. We had been out of touch for so long that we didn't know what to talk about outside of the children. Then, date night began to add financial strain. Even with researching, pre-planning and discounts it was still very expensive to go out every week.

We began date night with the intention of spending more time together. However, we discovered soon after it began that we were making it about trying to make up for lost time. This was incorrect and an unproductive way of thinking. There is no way humanly possible to "make up" for anything from the past. We should acknowledge it, ask for forgiveness (if applicable), and grow from it. We learned from our experiences that if you want to have a successful date night, you must plan for it. I define a successful date night as one that is stress-free, drama-free, argument-free and FUN!! You never want to end any date night feeling guilty about how much money was spent or feeling as if the time was not well-spent either.

So, with that said, here is my recipe for a successful date night.

D – Destination

A – Affordable

T – Time

E – Entertainment

DESTINATION:

It does not matter where you go. The only thing that truly matters is that you are together. Try to pick a place that you both will enjoy. If you cannot agree on a location, stay in! There is nothing like a quiet evening at home. If you are parents, the trick to having a date night in versus out is NO KIDS ALLOWED! Nothing ruins a moment like a screaming child or them asking you 50 times for a cup of juice. You should try to secure a sitter to take the kids out, set the atmosphere, and discuss ahead of time what you would like to do. Things can go left if one person wants to lay in bed together and watch a movie and the other person wants to organize the pantry. There is nothing wrong with both. The key is to make sure that both parties are on the same page.

AFFORDABLE:

There are plenty of things to do that are totally free! As previously stated, nothing ruins a date night like guilt from too much money being spent. I cannot stress enough the importance of pre-planning. Spontaneity went out of the window (for the most part) when we had kids. That does not mean that you give up on being spontaneous. You just plan for it! Make sure you have a couple of babysitters in your back pocket so when you do decide to be spontaneous, you aren't relying on one person to always be available. Look for coupons online. Give up the morning run to Starbuck's. Cut back on eating out for lunch and pack one instead. In other words, identify ways to save money for date night to avoid post-date-night guilt and to have some reserve funds for a spontaneous date.

TIME:

God has such a sense of humor! He gave me to someone who is anal about time and I have the tendency to be running a few minutes behind almost all the time! Therefore, I have learned that time is everything. In planning for date night, some factors to consider are as follows:

- How much time are we going to need a sitter for?

- How long will we be out?

- How often will we go out?

The first two questions may seem redundant; however, they are quite different. The first question may include time to get dressed and preparation for going out. You might not be able to get dressed in a timely manner with kids hanging off of you and demanding things every two seconds. If you do not have children, it could be the tv or the computer that may be a distraction, especially if you work from home. The second question includes travel time to-and-from home. The third question is to set expectations in effort to avoid disappointment and disagreements. Decide if date night will be once per week or once per month. It may even need to be every other month. You should decide as a couple what is right for your friendship, family, and finances.

ENTERTAINMENT:

What will you do on your date? Renting a Redbox movie, popping some popcorn, and staying in may be sufficient. Don't be afraid to keep it simple. Simplicity can lead to the creation of symmetry which can spark the chemistry that leads to intimacy. If you are a couple who stay in all the time, don't be afraid to try something new and different. What did our parents tell us growing up when we were afraid to taste a new food item? You don't know if you like it until you try it. My husband and I tried a few new activities and realized we did not like some of them. So, we said we won't do that again! No harm, no foul. We were together, we agreed to try it, and it was okay that we didn't care for it. On our path of trying new things, we discovered some activities we DO like, so those are the things that we choose to do when we don't have time to research something new.

Decide ahead of time how you will handle prioritizing date night. Research has shown that couples who still go out on dates together are happier and stay together longer than couples who do not. My takeaway from that is, date night should be a priority. But, consider this. If one person had a very long week and are too tired to follow through with date night, how will you handle it? Will the expectation be to muscle through it and go anyway? Or will you compromise and say you know what? Let's take a rain check or let's revamp this date night and stay in instead? Whatever you decide should be mutually agreed upon. This goes back to destination, affordability, time, and entertainment.

Discuss whether you will allow flexibility in going out versus staying in, how much money should be spent, how often you will have date night, and what you will do on your date. For ideas and detailed date night tips, visit my website www.igniteitright.org.

Last, but not least, NO TALKING ABOUT THE KIDS! My husband and I have made an agreement that there is to be no discussion about any one of our children. We have been out to eat at a restaurant several times and ran into people that we know. When they asked us about the kids, we replied by saying, "what kids?" Of course, they look at us as if we have fallen and bumped our heads, but so what! Date night is our time and we choose not to bring the kids for a reason. People who know us well know not to even ask us now. It's quite comical, but it is important. Remember, when we make it to retirement and the kids are all grown and gone, we still need to be able to have something to talk about. Training for that day begins now. For us, it began with committing to no "kid talk" during date night. Begin to think about and share the commitment(s) you are willing to make to one another.

All relationships require work, even friendships. With that said, the same DATE principal should be applied. Most people have busy lives and it is a sacrifice to set time aside to hang out with your friends. So, if all parties involved agree to spend time together it should be meaningful and respectful of everyone's time. There is nothing more stressful than finally getting together and feeling as if the time spent was wasted because there wasn't a plan in place. Also, if there was too much money spent it can affect households by causing financial strain or upsetting significant others. If there is a mate and children involved, staying out significantly later can stress out the person at home. So, being considerate of the time is helpful too. Remember, you are going out because you need a break and they do too.

There is nothing more attractive to me than a daddy taking his daughter out on her first date. It is my belief that fathers teach their daughters what their expectations should be of a potential mate. Dads set the tone for what her real dates should look and feel like. She should be respected, valued, and appreciated. No one else in the room should have his attention. This is the "feel." The car door and building doors should be opened for her, chair pulled out if at a restaurant, and he should return her home at or before her curfew. He should walk up to her door and come inside to pick her up and walk her to her door at the end of the evening. This is the "look."

Just as my husband will be my daughter's first date, I was my son's. No one knows how females desire and deserve to be treated better than another female! So, I was there to coach my son through it. You can learn a lot about how a man will be with a woman by the way he treats his mom. Therefore, my boys have been and will continue to be raised to treat all women with respect, care, and love.

My husband and I are old-fashioned when it comes to this whole dating thing. You do what works for you in your home. The key point is that parents are to date their kids first to set the example for their future dating behaviors.

Communicate Consistently

"Be gracious in your speech. The goal is to bring out the best in others in a conversation, not put them down, not cut them out." - Colossians 4:6

When couples stop talking, they also stop listening. How do you know how things are going or how each other feel if you aren't talking? How will your spouse know what your wants, needs, and desires are if you don't communicate them? Research has shown that lack of effective communication is one of the main causes for divorces. Some experts say that couples need to tell each other everything because that is the only way to work out all your problems. If you don't tell your spouse there is a problem, how can it be worked out? I remember a time in my marriage where I would hold things in.

I would be hurt or upset about something and not talk to my husband about it, but instead walked around with an attitude. He began to call me on it and then I began to tell him everything. But, some things did not need to be shared. There were some things that had nothing to do with my husband and everything to do with some internal issues I needed to deal with on my own. We discovered that I wasn't the only one who was holding things in. My husband was doing it too, but minus the obvious attitude. His was much subtler than mine. After many, many silly arguments, we began to practice the art of staying quiet, reflecting, and praying before we brought something forward for discussion. It gave us time to weed out the mess, deal with emotions, and organize our thoughts. This allowed us to have far more productive conversations.

Two key factors in effective communication are respect and trust. Couples must respect each other enough not to say mean or hurtful things intentionally no matter how angry or hurt they are. Tone and volume are equally important. There should not be any yelling, if possible. Avoid argumentative, aggressive, and sarcastic tones. This only fuels the flames to messy arguments. I have found that I can tell my husband almost anything. But, *how* I say it completely dictates how he receives it. *When* I decide to discuss things with him is crucial as well. I don't need to bombard my husband with my "honey-do-list" as soon as he walks through the door from a hard day at work. I have learned to allow him time to relax for a bit and then he will come to me when he is ready to talk. Clearly if it is something that is urgent that needs to be addressed right away, that is different. We both understand that sometimes business needs to be handled, so we give each other a pass.

Regarding trust, here is the story about married couple Talkative Tara and Silent Sam. Talkative Tara liked to talk, talk, talk. She told Silent Sam *everything!* If he hurt her, she told Sam and he listened. If he upset her, she told Sam and he listened. If he made Tara happy, she told Sam and he listened. If he annoyed her, Tara told Sam and he listened. This sounds okay, right? There is communication happening, right? Wrong! Silent Sam spent so much time listening that he was never the one speaking. Talkative Tara talked so much that she completely drowned out Silent Sam. In fact, she talked so much that even when Silent Sam mustered up the nerve to try to talk back, Talkative Tara talked over him and was rude to him at times. That's how Sam got his name. He got so tired of being disrespected and fighting to be heard, over time he just stopped talking.

This went on for years. But eventually, Silent Sam grew tired of listening all the time and never speaking.   One day Talkative Tara was doing her usual…talking, talking, talking. But this time Silent Sam snapped! (Another example of the volcano effect.) Silent Sam yelled, "ENOUGH! SHUT UP, TARA AND LISTEN!" Tara was so taken aback by his outburst that she quickly clamped her lips shut with her eyes stretched and arms folded.

Silent Sam began to tell her how he was tired of listening to her all the time and her never listening to him. When she realized how doing all the talking and never listening affected Silent Sam, she began to cry. She pleaded with him to forgive her and vowed to never ignore his thoughts and feeling ever again.

She also promised to do a better job with nit-picking. She learned that she did not have to point out every one of Silent Sam's wrongdoings, nor he hers. But instead, they could give each other the benefit of the doubt and chose to believe whatever was done was not done intentionally or out of spite. She realized they weren't enemies. She understood that opponents do not win! Tara also learned it was okay to let some things go. Proverbs 17:9 (NIV) says, *"Whoever would foster **love covers** over an offense, but whoever repeats the matter separates close friends."* They decided they didn't want to lose their friendship. Silent Sam forgave Talkative Tara and they both agreed to trust each other to honor their new commitments to one another. Talkative Tara promised to listen more and talk less. Silent Sam agreed to talk more and listen less. They lived happily ever after. The end.

What did this story have to do with trust? Well, Talkative Tara did not trust that Silent Sam was doing all the things that hurt, upset, and annoyed her unintentionally. She also did not trust him when he promised to try not to repeat the same mistakes that she pointed out. Silent Sam did not trust Talkative Tara's ability to listen to him. He also did not trust her to be respectful of his thoughts and feelings should they not agree with hers. So, they both had to learn to trust each other. They took baby steps one day at a time. Peace within their relationship was ultimately more important than pointing out flaws. They realized that their love for one another would not allow them to be disrespectful or hurtful toward one another. I Peter 4:8 says, *"Above all, have fervent and unfailing love for one another, because **love covers** a multitude of sins [it overlooks unkindness and unselfishly seeks the best for others]."* When I am seeking the best for my husband, I don't have time to focus on what he has done *to me,* but what I can do *for him.*

As with couples, when friends get into conflict it is usually due to an error in communication. Someone misunderstands the other or there were unrealistic expectations. Sometimes friends do not communicate their feelings to one another out of fear for hurting one another's feelings. It also could be due to a lack of desire for confrontation. Perhaps they have never been shown how to communicate effectively or efficiently.

Trust is also necessary in friendships. Friends need to know that they can trust each other to do no harm intentionally. I don't know about you, but I know without a doubt that I can trust my friends with my deepest, darkest secrets. I can share my heart with them. This does not mean that I have never been hurt by any of my friends. What it means is that I know in my heart and mind that neither one of them would intentionally do anything to hurt, upset, disrespect, or betray me or my trust.

I went through a very difficult time in my life and none of my closest friends were there for me in the way that I expected them to be there for me. Our relationship negatively changed for a time as a result. I later discovered that my friends did not know how to be there for me nor did I communicate how I wanted or needed them to be there. Had they asked what was needed or I told them what I needed, conflict could have been avoided. But, I do not in any way regret that experience. I learned how to be vocal about my expectations, wants, and needs. I also learned about the importance of avoiding making assumptions. We can't assume people know how we feel or what we need. We must tell them.

Analyzing why my kids did not get certain things done in the home or why certain things were done at school revealed a lack of communication. They did not fully understand the expectations because they were not communicated to them properly. Children have feelings and parents are not perfect. Children need to be able to trust their parents to feel comfortable sharing their feelings, wants, and needs. They need to know their parents aren't going to fly off the handle or use information shared against them. For example, if you lose it because your kid shares with you that they didn't turn in a homework assignment, how can they trust you not to lose it if they tell you they are thinking of having sex for the first time? Communication is the key to unlock confusion. But, no communication will consistently occur without trust.

TIP #6

Obey Unconditionally

"Lead good people down a wrong path and you'll come to a bad end; do good and you'll be rewarded for it." – Proverbs 28:10

In an internet search, I found this definition of the word obey, "comply with the command, direction, or request of (a person or a law); submit to the authority of." Some couples accept the philosophy that the husband is the head of the household and some do not. In an effort to avoid anyone getting all uptight, we will focus on the "request" part of the definition. If I request something from my husband or he something from me, we both have the expectation that the other will honor that request. Let's also focus on the "direction" part of this definition. I know that one strength of my husband is dealing with numbers. He was a mathematics major in college for goodness sake. This is not an area of strength for me. Therefore, I follow his direction as it pertains to our finances. One of my strengths is handling my son with special needs' medical bills. I have a degree in Medical Insurance Billing and Coding for Pete's sake. Who is Pete? No one knows! Anyway, I digress. Because I am an expert in this area, my husband yields to my direction.

Now that sounds nice, sweet, and simple enough. But, why are so many couples struggling with obedience then? I will tell you why. Obedience means being submissive to another's will. Not our own individual will, but someone else's will. We often have our own agendas. Many couples get married but never become one. The husband continues to do his own thing and the wife continues to do her own thing, never putting their two things together to make one big thing. It can be difficult to step outside of oneself and focus on another person. This can also be challenging when you have your first child. However, it is easier to do with your child than your spouse. This is because infants demand attention and care because they cannot do anything for themselves, whereas most adults are self-sufficient. Yielding to another's will begins with God. If we practice being submissive to His will, surely we can become submissive to another person's will.

If you truly believe what goes around comes around or that you should treat others the way you want to be treated this should become easier with time. While I am focused on taking care of my husband and he on taking care of me, we both end up being taken care of. Focusing on your spouse prevents you from falling into selfishness and resentment. It isn't healthy to fight against each other. You should always be working toward building up your relationship, not tearing it down. Obeying one another shows strength and humility. It also exemplifies love and respect for one another. But, boy is it hard!

When a person is accustomed to being in charge and the only one they must consider, it is challenging to release that. Allowing my husband to handle all the bills was a relief, but having to discuss what I spent was a headache. It felt as though I were a child asking for permission from my daddy. Everything comes down to our mentality and/ or thought processes. I agreed to "follow his direction" as it pertained to the finances. Therefore, I had a little talk with myself. I said, "If you say you trust him, then do it!" I learned that I couldn't trust him with some aspects of our finances, I had to trust him with all aspects of our finances. We did agree to compromise in some areas after I communicated my concerns. Overall, I trusted him then and I still trust him now to be the authority and the expert as it pertains to our financial goals and future.

Perhaps finances aren't an issue in your relationship. Maybe it is the other way around in your home in that the female is better with finances. Whatever the strength may be and whomever is better at something please just obey the authority of the more well-versed party. It can prevent a host of issues in your relationship.

One of my girlfriends is a very good driver and has excellent navigational skills. Therefore, when we go out I let her drive even if we are in my vehicle. This may seem small and that is okay. This doesn't have to be difficult. If I can listen to and submit to the direction of my GPS, why can't I do the same thing with my girlfriend who is a real person, tangible, and has my best interest at heart?

Sometimes I drive, but I still ask her to tell me the best way to go.

I know the Bible instructs children to obey their parents. I totally agree with this of course. Additionally, I believe that parents sometimes need to obey their children. Okay, okay take a deep breath! Don't throw the book away yet! At least hear me out first. What was the definition of obey? The definition of obey was to "comply with the command, direction, or request of (a person or a law); submit to the authority of." For example, if your kids "request" more responsibility to prove to you that they can handle it, you should obey (unless they have proven they aren't ready for what is being requested).

I have a teenager and he definitely is the authority regarding social media. So, you know what? I follow his lead and submit to his authority when I need to utilize social media or learn about the latest app. It may feel uncomfortable at first, but peace of mind is so worth it. Relax, rely, and release!

Verify the Source

"Do not secretly hate your neighbor. If you have something against him, get it out into the open; otherwise you are an accomplice in his guilt." –

Leviticus 19:17

Because marriage is God's design, it is virtually impossible to share information that has no biblical references. Often when there is an argument or conflict within a relationship, there typically is an underlying issue that is not being addressed. This appears to be the best time to discuss the Volcano Effect. Sometimes spouses do certain things that hurt or upset one another. And instead of discussing it, sometimes it is held in for days, weeks, months, and sometimes years even!

When a person is unaware of something they said, did, or didn't say or do, there is absolutely nothing they can do to correct or prevent repeating the offense in the future. Therefore, the person continues to repeat the same offense and the other person who is offended continues to say nothing. As this continues over time, the person who is offended gets angrier and angrier or even more hurt. This hurt or anger builds and builds up inside until the person explodes! Sadly, the person who has been holding in their offense typically explodes over something miniscule or something that really has nothing to do with why they are hurt or angry. The person who gets exploded on is usually confused as to why the explosion has occurred and may retaliate. Then, both parties are angry and possibly arguing. Time must then be spent de-escalating the situation and then discussing what caused the eruption in the first place.

Hopefully, once the couple moves past all of that, they can move on to discussing the underlying issue or issues. Nothing gets easily resolved using the Volcano Effect/Method, which is why I urge couples to discuss things as they happen versus holding their feelings inside. So, if there is a lot of arguing or tension between you and your spouse, try to identify the underlying issue(s) or verify the source.

Just as refusal to address underlying issues can be the source of confusion, it can also be a result of negative forces working against an individual or a couple. The first part of John 10:10 (AMP) says, *"The thief comes only to steal and kill and destroy."* I summarize that the enemy is attempting to steal, kill, and destroy the couples' joy. Sometimes, the enemy will use frivolous things to create discord amongst couples. He will encourage one person to keep his/her feelings hidden and the other person to ignore the signs of distress. These actions mutually can create conflict and division. The second part of John 10:10 (AMP) tells us that, *"[Jesus] came so that they [we] may have and enjoy life, and have it in abundance [to the full, till it overflows]."* Pray for God to help reveal the source of your conflict, unhappiness, disconnection, etc.

Verify the source if you are having strife in your friendships. Sometimes we try to hold onto relationships that are over. I truly believe that sometimes people are meant to be in our lives only for a time. When that time is up, we must let them go. When we do not, we will have strife. It is not always the case that the relationship is over, it could be there are unresolved issues which lead us back to communicating consistently. Sometimes as people we go through very stressful times and trying to find time to nurture our friendships may be more than we can handle at the time. Communicating this will typically prevent strife and facilitate compassion along with patience from the friend who may be feeling neglected.

We must also be mindful of the source when there is strife in our relationships with our children. Sometimes hormonal changes during puberty cause kids to be extra sensitive and incapable of communicating effectively. Smaller children may not have the words yet to articulate their feelings. They may be acting in unfavorable ways simply because they need more attention. As parents, if we are stressed about work or finances we can sometimes take this out on the kids. Maybe the child is stressed about schoolwork or had a fight with a best friend or someone they are dating and don't want to share that with you. Just one more thing might send them over the edge and they might blow up at you. This is not acceptable behavior, but I urge you to verify the source to increase your compassion, patience, and communication.

TIP
#8

Empty Hands =
Empty Hearts

"Give, and you will receive. Your gift will return to

you in full—pressed down, shaken together to make

room for more, running over, and poured into your

lap. The amount you give will determine the

amount you get back." − Luke 6:38 (NLT)

So, for many years I was accused of being materialistic. That could not be further from the truth! Do I enjoy nice things? Absolutely! But, it has never been about getting expensive things for me. It has truly been about the thought of me. I want to know that people I love and care about, are thinking of me. I have learned that "gifts" is in the top three of my love languages. It can be a flower that my husband picked up off the side of the road or a card that one of my kids handmade for me. I am not particular. But, I do enjoy just knowing that I was thought about at some point during my husband's day.

Before I knew about all this love language stuff, I used to give my husband gifts all the time. I never knew why he never appeared to appreciate it. I would get so disappointed and so frustrated because he never seemed excited by anything that I would give him. I would soon learn that we were speaking two different love languages. His primary love language is "acts of service." He would iron my clothes for work, do the laundry, and even try to prepare a meal (even though he was not as experienced in the kitchen as me) just so that I could have a moment to breathe. But then he would be disappointed and frustrated because I did not give him the response that he hoped for. I did not appear to appreciate it. So here we are the two of us both feeling unappreciated. We just couldn't seem to get on the same page.

Once we read and understood the five love languages everything changed. Not over night, but we saw consistent results. When I began to iron his work clothes and fix his lunch for him, I noticed that he began to bring home gifts for me. It was not easy for either one of us because we have different love languages and we had to put forth the effort to change. Boy, was it worth it! While I wanted tangible gifts, he wanted the physical gift of service.

There is no greater feeling than knowing that your spouse is listening and trying to make thing better. Never do anything that will cause financial strain because this can create unnecessary stress. This will defeat the whole purpose of trying to reignite the love/ passion in your marriage. Something will be ignited...anger! Learn what makes one another happy and make a consistent, continuous effort to do it.

When hands are empty or not moving, the heart feels empty too. Writing a short love note or picking up your spouse's favorite candy can truly brighten their day. Or taking the time to perform an act that you know they don't enjoy or feel up to doing, can truly fill the heart with love and joy. Moving hands signify active engagement in providing for the one you love to make them feel loved. Hands bearing a gift that cost $0 to one that costs $100,000 can create the same feelings…love, care, and concern. In essence, full (busy) hands truly do equal a full heart.

My girlfriend called me stressed out one day because she had a work event coming up and was overwhelmed by all the moving parts. I could not assist with the organization of the event, but I could lend my two hands the day of the event. All I did was show up and cook some hot dogs for the volunteers. I did not feel as if I did much. But, she told me had I not been there it would not have gotten done! Listening to your friends will present opportunities for you to fill their hearts. Make a conscious effort to make a friend's day using your hands. You can be a blessing by paying for a babysitter or agreeing to be the babysitter so that your friend can have a night out or in if they are too tired.

Be a blessing to your kids. Sometimes I dry my more-than-capable teenage son's clothes if he is in the middle of laundry, but I see he is busy doing homework or something else. I might iron his clothes for school or pick up one of his favorite snacks while I am in the store. I occasionally buy them all small gifts from the dollar store just because. I want them to know that I am thinking of them and that they are loved. Everybody has a desire to feel loved and these are just a couple of ways to do it.

TIP #9

Romance Regularly

"Love never ends." – 1 Corinthians 13:8

The minute some people hear the word romance, they automatically think about sex. According to dictionary.com, to "romance" means "to court or woo." In other words, you are attempting to win the favor, preference, or goodwill of someone and/or seeking to win the affection, or love, of that person. My suggestion is to court or woo regularly. If we are already married, don't we have favor, goodwill, love, and affection from our spouses already? Over time these things can fade. If you are reading this, my assumption is it is because of one of the following reasons: 1) Something faded, 2) You want to prevent something from fading, or 3) You want to make a good relationship even better.

There have been so many times where I have heard couples say they wish their mate would do the same things they used to do while dating. Does this mean that you must do EVERYthing you used to? Absolutely, not! I am not even sold on the idea that the person wants the exact same actions. I think it is all about the thought and the effort.

When I know that my husband took time to plan a date night, I am so moved. Even if I don't necessarily like the activity planned, I am still touched by his thought process and the effort that was made to do something nice and special for me.

As previously stated, couples should continue to date even though they are married. It keeps the passion and excitement alive in the relationship. After a long day or week, it gives a you as a couple something to look forward to. You can drown out all the noise from the world just for a little while to focus on connecting with each other.

Remember, if you have children, when you are spending time together, pretend as if you don't! I mentioned before that you don't have to duplicate all the things that you used to do for and with one another. However, there is beauty in the do-over.

You can show your partner that you remember the special moments or times together. Sometimes you don't have time or money to do anything big or extravagant. So, engaging in an activity that you previously did ensures that your spouse will enjoy it and you already know what to expect. Surprises can sometimes end badly if you plan something that your partner really does not enjoy. Let's be honest. We all get busy and are balancing a lot at one time. Therefore, we don't always have the time to research and plan something new. So, having that repertoire of previous date night activities can come in handy when you are crunched for time.

Courting or wooing your mate is not just about date night. While it is critically important, it isn't the only thing you can use to romance your spouse. Spend some time thinking about some of the little things you used to do for each other that you have ceased doing. What are some additional ways to woo your spouse? Can't think of anything? Well, that's why I'm here to help! See below.

- **Workout together.**

  ○ Taking care of your health is a great idea. It gets the endorphins going and ultimately puts you in a good mood. You guys can encourage and motivate each other during your workout. Successful couples want to feel supported. I don't know about you, but I want to know that my spouse has my back. My guess is you got married because you, along with many other people, enjoy being a part of a team. John C. Maxwell said "Team work makes the dream work..."

- **Take an unplanned day trip together.**

    ◦ Spontaneity makes people feel alive. It is so easy to get caught up in the mundane. So, just dropping everything and taking off can do wonders for your psyche and emotional health. Sometimes you just need to get away from it all and just focus on each other. You will return refreshed and reconnected; ready to take on the day.

- **Spend time just talking, sharing and listening.**

    ◦ Husbands want to feel heard just as much as wives. We all need to just stop, drop, and listen. You can't listen if you're speaking and you don't want to speak unless you're heard. Additionally, you aren't really listening if you are preoccupied with something else. The moments that are truly priceless are the ones when you can share your deepest and most interpersonal feelings. This is when couples truly connect with one another.

- **Thank your spouse for everything that they do for you and/ or the family by giving them a day off.**

  ○ Just by you giving the day off, you acknowledge that they do so much that they DESERVE it and have EARNED it. Try not to put too much emphasis on the "earned" part though. This may lead your spouse to think that they must do something in order to get something.

This isn't ultimately what you want. You want each other to know that you see them, hear them, and most importantly value them. This day off allows you the opportunity to care for them as they care for you. Besides, if you are working, most companies allow their employees time off. If your spouse is a homemaker or stay-at-home parent, they never get a day off. So, this tip is even more important in that scenario.

- **Play games like leaving notes around the house.**

  ○ As adults who have grown-up responsibilities, we sometimes forget how simple life used to be when we were kids. We didn't have to worry about anything, so we were carefree. We played games alone and with our friends and life couldn't be sweeter. Once you become an adult, life takes over and there are so many things one must consider or give attention to. We don't realize that even though we're adults, we still need playtime. Who better to play with than your spouse? You can leave notes that tell your spouse how much you love them or about what they mean to you. Should you decide to leave sexy notes remember to leave them in the bedroom only if you have kids who can't read. The sexy notes kill several birds with one stone. They can take your minds off more stressful things, let your spouse know that you were thinking of them, and can be used as foreplay. Board games or card games are also fun. To make it even simpler, try wrestling or a good game of Twister.

- **Pay attention to details (when your spouse mentions they want or need something, make a mental note to get it for them and surprise them with it.)**

  ○ This explanation seems like a no-brainer to me. Nothing says, "I'm listening when you speak" like this gesture. Not only were you listening to your spouse, but you make the extra effort to remember and patiently wait for the right time to act. If your spouse or you are like me, you enjoy surprises. So, not only am I feeling warm and gooey inside because my spouse was listening, took notes, and executed a plan, but I am also tickled pink because I got a surprise! For those of you who do not care about surprises, you still get the other benefits, just minus the surprise bonus. Your bonus could be your spouse surprising you before, after, or at the same time as you surprising them. Either way, this should be a win-win scenario. Remember, we don't give to receive. We give because it is the right thing to do. And we should get pure joy out of making our spouses happy.

- **Send sweet text messages during the time you're apart just to let your spouse know you are thinking of them.**

  ◦ Many places of employment do not allow employees to make or receive personal calls. Some careers are so fast-paced that one does not have time to breath, let alone make or receive a phone call. Other careers are dangerous and require complete focus leaving no time for phone calls, such as a 911 operator or emergency nurse. Whatever the case may be, there's nothing like receiving a nice text from your spouse in the middle of the day. It screams, "you are important to me" and "I miss you" along with notifying them that they were on your mind. This is healthy and adds fuel to your love reserves. For the person who has the fast-paced job or job that has other people's lives at stake, they will see the text whenever they take a break. That text might be just the thing they need to make it through the remainder of their shift, especially if they are having a rough day.

- **Spend a day in bed together.**

  ○ Don't take your pajamas off. Make breakfast in bed. Watch a good movie and pop some popcorn. Talk a little, but not too much. Sometimes you can get into discussing business matters which will add stress instead of removing it. Just spend time holding each other and if you fall asleep that's okay. Whether you have intercourse or not doesn't matter. What's most important is that you are shutting out the rest of the world just for a few hours to spend some quality time with your mate. No one or anything else matters on that day except the two of you.

I would be remiss if I did not mention something about sex. Sex, or intercourse, is simply another way to enjoy your spouse. Over time, sex can become boring and predictable. Sometimes couples get so busy that they neglect to make time for it. Some couples have been married for years, have not enjoyed sex with their mate, and chose not to share their truth. Let's face it. Sex, just like all other aspects of the relationship, must be cultivated and nurtured. It requires both parties to put in work to ensure that sex remains pleasurable, exciting, and fun. So, if you have been married for some time or recently married and are not enjoying sex, it is probably time to make some changes. Besides, did you get married not to enjoy sex? Absolutely, not! As absurd as that sounds, it's equally absurd for you to continue not enjoying sex and refusing to share that with your spouse.

Prior to trying anything new, it is very important to discuss the do's and don'ts with your spouse. Make sure that you both understand what is comfortable and uncomfortable. Your spouse is the main person that you should be able to be vulnerable with. So, be honest and do not judge. Spend time talking about your fears and fantasies. For example, you might say to your spouse, "I'm afraid to try _____ because I don't want you to look at me differently or "I'm afraid to _____ because I don't want you to expect it all the time or if I don't like doing it, I don't want to be held to doing it again just because you liked it." Open communication is critically important when you are about to introduce new things or acts into the bedroom. You should be able to trust your spouse not to do anything to hurt you and that they will respect your wishes. Try to keep an open mind and remember, no judgment! If you need ideas, visit an adult store or look for books at your local bookstore. Be careful with internet searches because they can turn up some things you aren't looking for!

Should you or your spouse have difficulty with arousal, performance, or interest please discuss it. Seek the advise of a medical professional if a dysfunction is suspected. It is equally important to avoid blaming yourself or your spouse. Sometimes, there is a medical reason why there's an issue. Sometimes, there is a lack of connection. Other times, it may just be due to boredom. But, talking openly with your spouse is critically important so that no one blames the other and so no one feels inadequate or insecure.

So, we are not going to use the same term to refer to friendships. We will use the "seeking to win the affection of another" part of the definition. If you truly care about your friends and value your friendships, you should want to make each other happy. We must nurture our friendships though. We have to spend time together in person and/ or over the phone. Thanks to technology, we can face-time or video chat using other means. In other words, there is no excuse for neglecting to communicate with friends. Like many things, it is all about the effort being put in. If you never speak or see one another, how can the relationship continue to grow? It can't!

When it comes to relationships with kids, they need time too. Therefore, we must make time to spend with our kids. We need to pour into these relationships as well. They need attention, affection, and love too. If you aren't sure about what is too much or not enough, just ask (if they are old enough to understand the question). One good thing about the relationship with kids is that the love is unconditional and there is no need for "attempting to win the favor, preference, or goodwill of (them) and/or seeking to win (their) affection, or love" because it's already there. However, making an effort to do so just makes their little love tanks overflow!

Support One Another

"Therefore encourage and comfort one another and build up one another…" – 1 Thessalonians 5:11

There is no greater feeling than knowing without a shadow of a doubt that your spouse has your back. My husband and I have each other's back. We support each other when we need to make decisions about whether our teenager can participate in certain activities, when we attend meetings with teachers, when we need to make career decisions, when we have conflict with others and more. We are never dishonest with one other, we always tell the truth, even when it hurts. Should there be an issue that occurs with another individual, we tell each other if we think the other party was in the wrong or if one of us was wrong. We bounce ideas off one another. I remember early in our marriage asking God why He gave me a husband who thought so differently from me. He was a math major in college and I was a psychology major. Math people see in black and white, whereas psychology people see shades of gray. It really used to annoy me how different my husband thought about things. Now, I embrace it. It still frustrates me at times because it isn't fun when we don't see eye-to-eye, but I certainly love it more than I hate it. He gives me a new perspective; one in which I probably never would have come up with on my own. It is a joy to have someone who has my best interest in mind, but brutally honest to be able to consult with and confide in.

Likewise, he had to make some very tough decisions over the years concerning his career and I was there to support him every step of the way. My husband was with a company for several years. He started at the company in a call center environment with a position that was supposed to be an 8-hour work day, but soon turned into a 14-hour day most days. He was coming home crashing from mental exhaustion. He wasn't any good to me or the kids. He was miserable. He eventually moved to a different department. This one was better than the first, but still very stressful. Eventually, the company closed that department and he was transitioned to a new department. He was okay there, but again it was very stressful as it was still a call center environment. So, I advised him to pray about it and I began to pray about it as well. I was specifically praying for favor and increase. He soon became a manager, which provided financial increase. His team was very successful and became recognized for their achievements. This in turn, made my husband look great and led to recognition, bonuses, and awards. God answered our prayers.

My husband was grateful, but had goals of moving further up in the company. So, I continued to pray for favor and increase. Nothing major happened. Over time, he realized he was with a company that afforded him little to no opportunities for further advancement. This eventually made him unhappy because of the professional goals he set for himself. One day, he received a call from a former co-worker who was recruiting him for the same position he was currently in at a new company. We prayed about it, he interviewed, and he was offered the position. So, he transitioned to the new company which is still where he resides today. He is so happy there! He was recognized for outstanding achievement within the first 6 months of being with the company, asked to lead a committee, and created a new format for an existing committee.

He has found favor. I kept wondering why it seemed that God was no longer answering my prayer. It wasn't that. It was just that God was ready to answer that prayer in a new environment. My husband was happy which is ultimately what we both wanted.

Transitioning to a new job is always difficult. But, this transition was very hard! My husband lost vacation time, certain benefits, and had to travel more. His hours were slightly different which meant he could not help with picking up the kids as much. His traveling meant I had increased duties and responsibilities. But, what am I supposed to do as a spouse? You guessed it! Support my spouse! So, I told him to do what he had to do. I would hold down the fort while he traveled and got settled into his new work home.

Equally, he was there for me when I transitioned to my current position. He supported me when I decided to become a Certified Professional Life Coach. Finally, he supported me when I told him I was going to be airing our dirty laundry in this book to help you! My husband and I have supported one another in many, many other ways. However, these are some of the highlights and most recent occurrences.

This is not extraordinary...this is exemplary. Supporting each other is a necessary component of a healthy, happy marriage. Supporting your spouse or them supporting you may not look exactly like this. It will look different for every couple. Support could look like not complaining if you need to start helping to cook dinner because your spouse decided to go back to school and has homework to do at night. Or support could be telling your friend(s) that you can't hang out as much because your spouse just had a baby and needs your help at home. The bottom line is, support means "to bear all or part of the weight of, give assistance to, or enable to function or act." Sometimes one person must bear all or part of the weight for the family. The examples that were shared above were examples of giving assistance (helping to cook) and/or enabling one to function or act (taking on more duties when the other pursues a new career/job). If no one else should have your back, your spouse should. So, be there for each other as often as possible. It will be inconvenient, but so is life at times.

It is equally important for friends to support one another. We should be there when times are good and bad. I know right now that if I had an issue, there are friends that I can call to help physically or just spiritually by praying for me. This is where nurturing your friendships comes in handy. If you only call a friend when you are need, they will not be as eager and willing to assist. Also, if you are never available when they need you, you may not receive a very warm reception. I am there for my friends when there are issues with spouses, financial difficulty, job stress, kids driving them crazy, or just typical lady stuff and they do the exact same for me. Luke 6:31 says, *"Do unto others as you would have them do unto you."*

The same philosophy applies to our kids. As parents it is our job to support them in every way- physically, financially, spiritually, emotionally and more. When kids do not get the support they need from home, they sometimes seek it out in the wrong way or from the wrong people. This is how kids sometimes get caught up in negative acts or negative relationships. Take some time to reflect on how your parents were or were not there for you. Mirror the positive ways they supported you and refrain from the negative ways they supported you. If there was no support at all, please make every effort you can to avoid repeating the same behavior. Kids equal sacrifice. Parents often must make sacrifices to ensure their kids have a healthy, happy life. In the end, it is more than worth it.

Parenting a Child with Special Needs

Having a child with special needs has been wonderful and rewarding, but at the same time exhausting and disheartening. Because we have a child with special needs, we have met some extraordinary people and traveled to places we probably never would have gone. We almost lost our son, so every day that he wakes up is a great day. Again, we have learned not to take anything for granted as tomorrow is not promised to any of us. This should translate into our marriages as well. Because tomorrow is not promised, we must enjoy every day that we have with our spouses. We cannot allow small, trivial miniscule things to cause dissension within our relationship. Just as we should view our children as gifts, so should we view our mates. Some of our best times have been **laughing out loud** while playing with our son with special needs and **enjoying each other's** company. He has brought so much joy to our family with his addictive laugh and gorgeous dimpled smile. We wouldn't be complete without him.

When we brought our son home from the hospital, he had a feeding tube, VP shunt, hearing and vision impairments, 6 new specialists, and a bag full of medications. It was disheartening seeing our son who was once very vibrant, be docile, immobile, and without effect. He has made significant improvements; however, help with self-care is still required. Having to bathe, clothe, feed, etc. a teenager is exhausting. There are many times when we don't agree on what is best for our son, but we **communicate consistently** and come to a decision together as a team because **opponents do not win.** We have identified our individual strengths and **obey** each other **unconditionally.** If my husband, the expert with finances, says we need to cut back because our son needs something, I do.

Caring for a child with special needs has many challenges. Between keeping up with doctor appointments, medicine, insurance changes, hospitalizations, therapy and more, we don't need any additional stress. Should there be conflict, we **verify the source** and deal with it accordingly. We avoid **empty hands** as we keep them busy by caring for our kids and each other. We focus on nurturing our relationships as we **romance regularly** to gain favor, goodwill, and affection from our son and each other. We support each other and our son which leads to **victory for all.**

As I am writing this book, we are going through a very challenging time with our son. He has self-injurious behaviors and over the past couple of months his meltdowns (as we call them) have increased in intensity, frequency, and duration all at the same time. It…is…hard! Trying to find time to eat, shower, clean, etc. is difficult enough, but trying to find time to write seemed virtually impossible at times. But, thank God for our village! Have you ever heard that saying, "it takes a village to raise a child?" Well, I firmly believe that. We have friends and family that help us out and we could not do what we do if it was not for them. Moral of the story, build up your village if you have not done so already.

While I shared with you many of our tribulations, our son with special needs does not care about any of these everyday struggles. It isn't our job to try to make him care. We just want him to have a happy, healthy life that is as normal as possible. The thing that matters to him the most is love, because truly *love covers.*

Brush Fires

As previously stated, I am not the resident expert. However, I have experienced many things in my marriage that have taught me so many life lessons that I thought would be helpful to share with you. Many people enter marriage with unrealistic expectations. This is the reason I highly recommend going to pre-marital counseling. If you are already married, that is okay too because you can go afterward. Even if you went to pre-marital counseling, got married but are having some issues in your marriage, you can go to counseling anytime that you feel necessary. I truly believe there is nothing too hard for God. I firmly believe that if you and your spouse allow yourselves to be open, vulnerable, and really try to be better and do better, you will. Do all that you can within your own might, give everything else over to Him, and God will work it out. Counseling should serve as a guide to help you improve your relationship. This book was not meant to be a religious one, however as previously stated, it is impossible to talk marriage and not mention God because it is His design. Couples often have issues because they are not executing the correct formula. They are missing one very important ingredient…God.

If you adopt all the tips that were shared, I believe you can and will have a happy, healthy marriage. "Adopt," is an action word. This insinuates there is something you must do. That would be correct because marriage takes work. Not just work by one, but work by both parties involved. You must not overwhelm yourselves, but take one day at a time. Everything will not, nor can it be fixed overnight. It is a gradual process that requires commitment, dedication, patience and perseverance.

As previously mentioned, our son with special needs has self-injurious behaviors. We managed it for a time, but eventually we needed help. So, we contacted a behavioral specialist. They taught us that some of our responses to his behavior were reinforcing the unwanted behaviors. They taught us new, more appropriate responses. With our commitment to the plan, dedication to seeing things through, patience, and perseverance until we saw change, his behavior eventually improved. Our son did not like our new responses, so his behaviors escalated. Things got worse, before they got better. This may be the same with your marriage. When you begin to respond differently to the challenges in your marriage, things may get worse before they get better. We tend to fall back on what we're used to because it is familiar, even when it isn't good for us. But, if you just hang in there and trust God, you will see change for the better.

Now you have the tips. You have the most important ingredient. There is one final thing you must also keep in mind. If you do not love yourself, it is virtually impossible for you to love anyone else.

Likewise, if you aren't happy as an individual, it is

unfair for you to expect your spouse to make you

happy. I was involved in a couple of relationships

prior to my husband that were abusive in various

ways. Because of situations that occurred in those

past relationships, I did not recognize my worth. I

didn't love myself and I took it out on others around

me. I was filled with so much anger and hurt that I

wasn't ready to forgive myself (and the others that

hurt me), let alone love myself. Through prayer and

through others showering me with love, I overcame.

I eventually forgave, repented, began to recognize

my worth, and began to love me. Does that mean

that I am completely satisfied with everything that is

me? NO! I am not perfect. Therefore, there is

always room for growth. I continue to pray and ask

God to help me to be a better version of myself. It is my desire to be a better person for me first. I also desire to be a better wife, mom, sister, daughter, friend, cousin, niece, etc. Ultimately, the more I love me, the more I can love others.

Before I became happy on my own, I used to expect my husband to make me happy. I would get angry with him because he wasn't making me happy. He felt defeated because nothing he did seemed to make me happy. It was an impossible feat. Making me happy with myself was not his job. This was something I had to resolve on my own. Once I learned that, it enabled me to take some of the pressure off of him. Then, he could just focus on loving me. I thank God for my husband. I would not be the woman I am today had it not been for him. I didn't believe it in the beginning, but I know now without a doubt in my mind that God knew exactly what He was doing when he put the two of us together.

There are going to be times when you and your spouse do not like each other. There will be times when you don't agree. There may even be times when you feel like you don't love each other. It is so easy to get caught up in the mundanities of married life that we sometimes forget about the romance and even stop working on our relationship. To prevent that from happening, apply the tips you have learned in this book. If you are already there, apply the tips from this book. There is nothing impossible for two people who put 100% of their individual energy into improving their relationship. It is my prayer and my desire that this book will spark a brush fire in your marriage that is never extinguished, but instead continues to burn forever. That the passion and love in your marriage will continue to burn for each other more and more, so much so that your light will shine so brightly that all will see.

Likewise, when we do not love ourselves it is almost impossible to have healthy friendships or healthy relationships with our children. Therefore, I urge you to work on yourself if you have identified personal areas of opportunity. No matter how tough things get or how dismal things may appear, remember that *love covers!*